Edgy Poetry

Edgy Poetry

Marlene Mesot

Independently published

Editing, print layout, e-book conversion,
and cover design by DLD Books

DLD Books

www.dldbooks.com
Editing and Self-Publishing Services

Cover photo by Marlene Mesot

© 2020 by Marlene Mesot
All rights reserved

ISBN: 978-1-7347393-4-3

4 Elements of Mystery Series

1. The Purging Fire
2. The Snowball Effect
3. Whirlwind of Fear
4. Terra Terror

More Mysteries

The Cat Stalker's Sonnets — novel

Poetry

Edgy Poetry
The Author's Edge

www.marlsmenagerie.com

Dedication

This work is dedicated to all my friends and fellow writers who belong to Behind Our Eyes Writers' Group. Thank you sincerely for your constructive criticism, encouragement and true dedication to our writing craft. May God bless and productive writing.

Table of Contents

Edgy Poetry Introduction 9
Sleepless Night.. 10
Questions of Mystery 11
Absurd.. 12
Rocking Chair Talk 13
When My Aunt Died... 14
Emotions 15
Curiosity 16
Bad Omen.. 17
Bread of Dreams 18
Balloon Phobia... 19
The Purging Fire 20
Colorful Feelings 21
FEAR.. 22
In the Forest of the Night 23
In the Woods.. 24
The Night Before... 26
Nameless Feeling.. 27
Despair 28
Disaster 29
Doom.. 30
Not Beautiful 31
Without Warning... 32
The Edge of Your Mind... 33
Cloudy with a Chance of Uncertainty................................... 34

Escape	35
The Crash	36
Storm	37
Bump in the Night Sonnet	38
In the Still of the Night	39
About the Author	40

Edgy Poetry Introduction
(Quatrain)
06/06/2020

This work is not for the faint of heart,
Or for reading in the dark.
To the reader I make a pledge.
This is poetry with an edge.

In that slow, uncertain time,
When you need something to unwind,
You might ponder whether to tread
Through these pages with an edge.

Not to frighten or demean,
Nor to stir up the unseen,
Not to strain the ear to listen,
Not to cause the sweat to glisten,

Upon your hand as the page you turn.
Nor to make your stomach yearn
For the feel of comforting peace
As through these pages you do leaf.

Not to cause your mouth to dry,
Nor to feel a wet tear cry.
Just to give you room to hedge
Through this poetry with an edge.

Sleepless Night
(Limerick)
07/05/2020

The night was hot. I couldn't sleep.
Had no promises to keep,
Went outside to see.
Air was still. No breeze.
Then, a sound, someone to peep?

Questions of Mystery
(Sextet)
06/21/2020

What fascinates us about mystery?
Why has it endured throughout history?
Who watch movies that scare?
Where to accident scenes people flock to stare?
When will curiosity cease to care?
How will it resolve, the mystery?

Absurd
(Short Couplet)
06/13/2020

Gloom and doom in a room is a rhyme.
Although it may seem unkind,

Without meaning and purpose,
Writing is useless and worthless.

Writing has worth—
Even with mirth.

So take it seriously.
Don't squander it deliriously.

A poet is one who takes a word
To arrange it in the absurd.

Words have a way, to form a display,
Of thought patterns, in an array.

Rocking Chair Talk
(Short Couplet)
06/13/2020

Rickety rock, crickety crock
The rocking chairs talk

As bones old and brittle
Seek solace in their middle.

Close relatives cry
As time passes by

Knowing that when
Now becomes then

Their loved one will pass
To become memories at last.

When My Aunt Died
(Short Couplet)
06/06/2020

Have you ever experienced the feeling of déjà vu?
First gone to some place that suddenly you knew?

If you've ever awoken from a bad dream
To find it real...You wanted to scream!

It happened to me at age eleven.
I woke to find my aunt went to Heaven.

Though healthy and active I dreamed she had died.
Next morning Dad told me she was no longer alive.

She'd had a stroke. Died suddenly. No fight.
The sinister call came around midnight.

NOTE: True story.

Emotions
(Limerick)
06/15/2020

Soft as a cat in the fog,
Hard as an old prickly log,
Wayward, shifting, flat,
Changing just like that,
Emotions can bog the dog.

Curiosity
(Sextet)
06/21/2020

What killed the cat without thought?
What trouble brings on our plot?
What makes us brave 'til end fraught?
Dubiosity.
Curiosity.
Our best laid plan to end—thwart.

Bad Omen
(Trident)
06/13/2020

From superstition,
Even though we petition,
There is no remission.

From something sinister
There is no warning altimeter,
No protective perimeter.

When it comes to bad omen,
There is no roamin',
To escape the charlatan.

Bread of Dreams
(Acrostic Sextet)
06/21/2020

Dreams mix in sticky like dough.
Reality rising,..identity lost in the bowl.
Eggs of encounters bind and thicken.
Add uncertainty, stir, and quicken.
Memories pour in to loosen the fold.
Seeds of sanity lost to my soul.

Balloon Phobia
(Sonnet)
07/05/2020

Imagine standing in the middle of a room,
Filled with squeaky, creepy balloons.
From floor to ceiling there is no room,
Because it is packed with hovering balloons.

Now imagine a nightmare,
Where you stand naked in fear.
There is no room anywhere,
As to your skin balloons adhere.

Standing barefoot there is no escape,
Any move may cause them to pop.
All you can do is stand there and gape.
They flutter and squeal around and on top.

Finally you startle awake!
Only a dream to escape.

NOTE: I have had a balloon phobia, since I was little. I have had this repeating dream, fortunately, not frequently.

The Purging Fire
(Quatrain)
09/28/2011

The Purging Fire burns aright.
No one can reach beyond its blight.
The Purging Fire cleanses all.
There's no escape beyond its wall.

The Purging Fire. Feel the heat.
Flames of desire, no one can beat.
The Purging Fire breathes defeat.
It judges all within its reach.

The Purging Fire. No one can win.
It purifies. It judges sin.
The Purging Fire. To it we'll fall,
It's flaming mass consumes us all.

NOTE: This poem has one more verse relating to my book The Purging Fire, *the first book in the* 4 Elements of Mystery *series.*

Colorful Feelings
(Couplet)
06/06/2020

Red rage of anger boils quite a lot,
As the sting of cinnamon candy red hot.

Blue pain of tears tightens the throat,
As much as dry meat makes you choke.

Green touch of envy is nothing pretty.
Spinning the mind with yarns to make you dizzy.

Indecisively orange between red and yellow,
Is tasteless and useless like melon mellow.

Purple restraint brings black and blue,
As tart as lemon and purple grapes, it is true.

FEAR
(Acrostic)
06/13/2020

Frightfully fragile as fleeting, foggy thoughts,
Eerily echos as silence,
Acrid tastes of acid in the throat,
Rapidly, relentlessly rising as a raging storm, is fear.

In the Forest of the Night
(Quatrain)
06/06/2020

In the forest of the night,
Unknown sounds might give you fright,
Unless you are knowledgeably aware
Of nocturnal creatures out of their lair.

Step with caution as you move
Across slippery leaves, tangled twigs and rocks smooth.
Notice the direction of the babbling brook,
Lest you slip off an overlook.

In the forest of the night,
Ponder your reason for the flight,
Before you come upon unaware…
A lion, a tiger or a bear.

In the Woods
(Quatrain)
09/10/2015

Whether for ill or good,
I found myself in the woods.
Whether lost or found,
I couldn't escape, trees all around.

10/17/2015

In the woods the breeze sighs softly what it knows.
Thoughts skitter among the branches to and fro.
Secrets burrow beneath blankets of leaves or snow.
In the woods, no one knows.

In the woods dreams fly across the clearing wild and free.
Until reason snares them like the roots of an aged tree.
Uproot and unearth these creatures into infinity.
In the woods.

Marlene Mesot

05/18/2016

Leaves of red, yellow and gold,
Scatter with anger, fear and loath.
Branches become barren and lifeless
In the woods.

NOTE: This poem introduces the short story "One Weekend...in the Woods," first published in Trusting In God: Stories That Inspire, *Various Authors, Christian Book Marketing (9 October 2019) Volume 7. p. 65.*

The Night Before…
(Quatrain)
06/06/2020

'Twas the night before rescue or ruin.
I found myself standing, mentally stewin',
In a one room cabin with fireplace aglow
Against the wind, cold and blanket of snow,

That spread through the landscape of woods outside.
This small refuge was the only place to hide.
Somehow I became separated, lost to my friends,
Whom I sincerely wished no bad end.

Now as I stood pondering my plight,
I heard a swoosh of snow falling in the night.
Then came a thud as if something at the door.
Rescue or ruin, I wondered, on that night before…

Nameless Feeling
(Cross Rhyme Quatrain)
06/15/2020

Soft as a shiver,
Cold as a chill,
Prickly as a sliver,
Silent and still.

Acrid as acid settling in the stomach,
Heart hammering hurriedly,
Body temperature can plummet—
Suddenly.

That nameless feeling sears.
It crawls and creeps,
Leers and jeers—
Inside your head it peeks.

Despair
(Limerick)
06/13/2020

Tread softly upon the floors.
Don't attempt to open doors,
Where curious things
Lurk in shadows, brings
Despair, and hardship it pours.

Disaster
(Trident)
06/13/2020

It is said disaster comes in threes,
Sneaking softly as a summer breeze
Slipping silently among the trees.

It steals your now, your future, your breath.
With memories you are left
To fathom the consequences…bereft.

When it strikes there is no laughter—
No before, no after,
No accounting for disaster.

Doom
(Alliterative Quatrain)
06/13/2020

Between the black and the white,
Between the darkness and the light,
Between whispering waves and surging surf,
There is a place of uncertain turf.

Where shapes are formless,
Where time is endless.
Uncertainty dwells—
Casting its spells.

This place is in twilight
With no wrong and no right.
Covered in gloom
It predicts doom.

Not Beautiful
(Quatrain)
07/05/2020

Oh beautiful, for shining eyes,
And creepy noises too,
For hidden things, reflective blings,
In the sky not blue.

For creepy, crawly night creatures,
For ticks and bats, and hidden traps,
Let's leave this place. It's no disgrace.
To be safely home under wraps!

Without Warning
(Quatrain)
06/13/2020

This is not a limerick,
Nor a riddle or acrostic.
This is just a poem written in the morning,
Written without warning.

The mind is a place clever,
Where the writer chooses to endeavor,
To piece together in place
A work, at a frantic pace.

Some thoughts that swarm in the head
May to the paper be dead.
Plans seemingly set in stone
Can change and sink like old bones.

From frightful darkness into the light,
There is no wrong. There is no right.
It was evening, and it was morning…
Without warning.

What goes into the heart, or into the head,
One source for new life, one source for the dead.
A poem written in the morning
Can change by night—without warning.

The Edge of Your Mind
(Quatrain)
07/05/2020

There is something there but you cannot grasp,
It is too impossible a task,
To climb,
To the edge of your mind.

When short-term memory is taken abruptly,
There is no way to prepare, not even roughly.
It seems so unkind,
To the windmills of your mind.

Thoughts twist and churn.
There is no way to learn,
How they came to be
Where chaos roams free.

When you search for something lost,
In your mind you turn and toss.
Why do you not recall,
And make sense of it all?

Cloudy with a Chance of Uncertainty
(Quatrain)
06/13/2020

Cloudy with a chance of uncertainty,
Wayward as storm of hesitancy.
Emotions waver with difficulty,
When indecision invites calamity.

As light as the mist of the fog,
Or heavy as dew on the bog,
As thick as the vapor of cloud,
Uncertainty shouts aloud.

As subtle as the first splash of rain,
It puddles out to increase pain.
Obscure as the vibration of thunder
Uncertainly rolls asunder.

Thickening like a covering of snow,
Rocking emotions to and fro,
Uncertainty twines in the stomach,
Sending confidence to plummet.

Escape
(Alliterative Quatrain)
07/05/2020

Wind rushing,
People crushing,
Sky gone gray,
No place to stay.

Pitter patter,
Hurry scurry,
Wet. No matter.
Escape the flurry.

Damp, chilly,
Trek hilly,
A treacherous way
To escape the fray.

Blizzard squalling,
People bawling,
Escape the swarm
To stay warm.

The storm is a blanket of snow.
The road is a long way to go.
Hold fast to your individual identity,
To escape the lunacy.

The Crash
(Couplet)
07/05/2020

Tires rumble.
Feet stumble.

Brakes squeal.
Legs reel.

Metal crashing.
Lights flashing.

Memory flees the aftermath—
Of the crash.

Storm
(Trident)
06/13/2020

Lightning flashes.
Thunder crashes.
Rain is imminent.

Patience crumbles.
Frustration rumbles,
When anger runs rampant.

Bump in the Night Sonnet
(Internal Rhyme)
06/13/2020

A sound in my head,
Nearly dampening my bed,
Creeping, crawling,
Barely bawling,

Ears alert,
Muscles hurt,
Heart palpating,
Sweat satiating,

Mouth nearly foaming,
Eyes rotating…roaming,
Stomach nauseous,
Footsteps cautious,

These are the signs of fright—
When something goes bump in the night!

In the Still of the Night
(Quintain)
05/04/2020

The night was hot. I couldn't fall asleep.
Although I had no promises to keep,
I went downstairs to see what I could see.
Outside my house the air was still. No breeze.
And then, a sound. Was there someone unseen?

Note: The first line of this poem was a prompt from a writing course with Creative Writing Now.

About the Author

Marlene Mesot, an only child, grandchild, and niece from Manchester, New Hampshire, and deceased husband, Albert, have two sons, two grandchildren, and English Mastiff dogs. She is legally blind and moderately deaf due to nerve damage at premature birth. She has loved writing since early childhood.

Marlene holds a Bachelor of Education degree from Keene State in Keene, New Hampshire, and a Masters in Library and Information Studies from UNC Greensboro, North Carolina.

www.ingramcontent.com/pod-product-compliance
Lightning Source LLC
Chambersburg PA
CBHW071506080526
44587CB00016B/2712